The Postcolonial Flâneuse

Ramisha Rafique

Five Leaves Publications

The Postcolonial Flâneuse
Ramisha Rafique

Published in 2025 by Five Leaves Publications
14a Long Row, Nottingham NG1 2DH
www.fiveleaves.co.uk
www.fiveleavesbookshop.co.uk

ISBN: 978-1-915434-33-3

Copyright © Ramisha Rafique 2025

Printed in Great Britain

Contents

Postcolonial Flâneuse	7
Being Muslim Women	8
Book in Hand	10
Café Soundtrack	11
Nottingham	12
Woman	13
Olive Trees	14
Coffee Shop, Milton Street	15
Nakbah in the West	16
I'll Tell You of the Boulevards	17
Stickers on Street Signs	18
Stranger	19
Tea	20
They Watch Pigeons Gather	21
For Those Lost in The Kashmiri Diaspora	22
Man	23
Turtle Walking in Flying Horse Arcade, Nottingham	24
Barista	25
The Ends of the Earth	26
Girl Talk	27
Musée de l'Absence	28
Mardi 21 Mars 2023, *Le Monde*, 3.40 €	29
Pavé	30
Le Coup de Foudre: Jardins du Luxemburg, 2 June 2022	31
Paris Metro	32
Rue	33
Red Chairs	34
Arab Quarter, Marseille	35
Parc du Champ de Mars	37
Rue St Honoré	38
Cession of Colonialism	39
Galata Bridge	40
Taksim	41
21,000 Steps	42
10km from Syria	43
Beşiktaş Port	44
Little Shops	45

Roasted Pistachios	46
Man Outside Coffee Shop	47
Tawaf in Lockdown	48
Cyber Flâneuserie	49
Ghost City	50
A Hashtag	52
War in 2024	53
Instagram Captions	54
Acknowledgements	55

Ramisha Rafique's poetry allows the reader to immerse themselves in the familiar and the strange, often at the same time. This is a sterling debut, timely in its updating of the role of flânerie and the all-important role of the poet in today's wider world. We need voices like this.

Andrew Taylor

A definition of simplexcity.
Narratives that not only disrupt, but literally set thought in motion.
Work that bubbles and froths in brooks of confluence.
Cultivated, delicate passages that engulf and defy, entice and restrain, carried along on a current of defiance and deference.
Truly a meeting of worlds on every page.

Paul Adey/ CAPPO

Ramisha's writing is a vivid reclamation of the flâneur's gaze. She dramatically flips the traditionally white, male, European voyeur's role inside out by not only wandering, but witnessing European metropoles. The poems hold an enjoyable, intimate and I want to say 'gentle' radicalness: A Muslim woman strolling through coffee shops, in city streets, subverting through her poetic observations. I felt that she took my hand and journeyed with me in a way that both comforted and exposed!

Suhaiymah Manzoor-Khan

*To my mother, who taught me how to
walk through the world with courage*

Postcolonial Flâneuse

'There is something maddeningly attractive about the untranslatable, about a word that goes silent in transit' – Anne Carson

No two gazes are the same. My presence, visible, noticeable, judged and assumed. I am another version of George Sand, hidden behind a camouflage of identity politics and pronoun wars. Anonymity isn't a privilege for all.

Invisibility in crowds of pedestrians, streets, bus stops, and coffee shop queues, pavement tables and library rooms. Is there a lack of me in the spaces I inhabit? You're socially aesthetic, Instagram grids, whatever fits, it follows the rage.

Neutral positions clash with colourful scarves and turbans, veils, bands, and bracelets. You can't tell them what not to wear, here. Is it my faith that is silencing me or your gaze? Is there a lack of me in the spaces I inhabit?

Give space. deep breaths, sighs, long strides, fingers fiddling in laps, chins resting in hands. Alhamdulillah. I can walk where I like.

Being Muslim Women

In the beginning there were just women.

Women who became women of class
of race
of nation
of religion.

Women who became women of
skin colour
skin type
hair colour
hair type.

Eye colour
leg lengths
waist sizes
chest sizes.

Still women.

Women who became career women.
Political women.
Racialised for hidden agendas.
A threat if they speak out,
have views of their own.

Muslim women.

Muslim women with
beliefs and opinions.
Who wear a hijab.
Who don't wear a hijab.
Straight, queer, non-binary.

Women.

Walk
and stroll
and think
and run
and resist
and stand
and exist.

Who did you get your assumptions from?

Book in Hand

She has become part of
the mass. She is him, and her,
and them.

She is the flow, sway,
and turn.

She stops to catch her breath.
Crowds continue to pass,
hair flying forward.

The seat next to a man smoking
a cigarette is vacant.

She finds herself beside a
steamed-up coffee shop window,
book in hand.

Café Soundtrack

Piano keys begin a slow melody.
Guitar strings, soft, stirring.

             Instrumental.

Conversations
between
individuals at tables.
Merging into lyrics.

             Break.

Sound of grinding coffee beans
and laughter from behind the counter.

Accents:
Yorkshire English.
Emirati Arabic.
Local Nottingham slang.

High notes transition to
mellow symphonies.

Cup clinks on saucer.
Rustling sugar sachet,
awkward eye contact shifts.

Confident glances across the room. A student grabs a hand full of
            white sugar to drown in their coffee.

Man fiddling with his rings.
Listening attentively.
Man in a blue cap walks past
the window eating a pasty.

            Outro.
         Steam
      floats
     from
    his
  mouth

into the cold air.

Nottingham

Wherever the flâneur or the flâneuse
is emerging the city is moving.

In passages, arcades, and
cobbled streets.
Search for it!

I walk down:
Heathcoat St.
Carlton St.
St. Mary's Gate.
Stoney St.
Bridlesmith Gate.

I find a familiar energy,
in its mosques of art,
temples of rebellion,
churches of uprising.

Woman

Woman standing at the bus stop,
wrapped in fast fashion.
You fight the strong wind
while waiting for a delayed bus.

Where will you go after a long day?
Overdue sleep seems to be catching
up to you.

Is it a short trip home or
do you have a few stops?

Weird men and loud teenagers
standing idle
outside fast-food restaurants
and takeaways.

You remain unbothered,
looking down
at your feet now.

Will you shut your eyes, just briefly,
when resting your head against the window?

Does the sound of rain drops
blowing against glass
block out the music
in your headphones?

Olive Trees

We're taught to read and write
a language that we cannot speak.

There are
no translations,

explanations,
or justifications.

We are told that this is
the only way to speak to God.

We read the letters and understand
The accents before we know what prayer is.

There are forms of meditation and supplication
but only the authorities can access their powers.

How do we reach a sanctuary when
we can't understand the signs that lead us there?

Coffee Shop, Milton Street

It's a Tuesday afternoon,
the café is almost empty.

Usually, it's crowded
and I struggle to get a seat.

Today, even conversations seem
hush hush.

Noise from the kitchen is loud,
cutlery clatters.

Glasses clink as they're
stacked on top of each other.

People leave whilst
others are just arriving.

Like musical chairs,
the room keeps changing.

Shuffled
and shuffled again.

Nakbah in the West

I

Thunder rumbles.
Birds tremble beneath thick branches.
The bush in the back garden
has lost all its leaves. It's summer.

The sky is the colour of mustard.
Clouds used to hover over us
around lunchtime, but now they
occupy the whole sky.

I can't move my feet.
The neighbour's cat hides
under my car. It thinks
it's found a safe haven,
but when the sky roars,
something rips beneath us.

II

Everyone on the street is asleep
but I'm in the road when it
begins to rain.

Hailstones like golf balls.
The rain is melting
away the street as we know it.
No one lets the cat back in.
The trees sink into cracks in the concrete.

I shout for help
but I can't hear my own voice.
Water rises around my ankles.

I'll Tell You of the Boulevards

after Andrew Taylor

Draw on the noise,
attached to vandalised
buildings and statues.

Ignored pieces of iron and stone
are enough now to commemorate the dead.

Someone will sleep against them.

Distance is finding,
in clusters of swaying hats,
your voice in theirs.

Echoing between both worlds.

In sitting still,
you will be moved in the right direction.

Andrew Taylor, 'Tell Me of the Boulevards', March, *(Bristol: Shearsman Books, 2019)*

Stickers on Street Signs

What is a sign if not a declaration –
inviting direction for change.

Despite interventions,
intentions for those who
walk past, not noticing.

People in these crowds
are communicating.

They are encouraging one
another to take action.
Resist.

Stranger

I hoped to see you sitting in the café already,
but you're not here.

I order my coffee and watch the people in the room,
the city moves on, but you don't show.

I'll wait for another unexpected encounter, then.
In a café somewhere around here.

Tea

Allow the leaves to sit a little longer.
Time will give flavour,
colour will follow.

They Watch Pigeons Gather

Man is standing on corner,
listening to music
through his headphones,
but not the city.

Woman standing in the Market Square.
Busy spaces. She listens to the rumble of buses,
people talking, trams whirring.
She is watching pigeons gather.

For Those Lost in The Kashmiri Diaspora

My friend tells me I cannot offend her.
Her skin colour was never used
to enslave or oppress her people.

Mine still is.

Girls in Jammu and Kashmir cannot walk through streets
or sit peacefully in cafes reading books.

Girls in Jammu and Kashmir tiptoe through military zones
on their way to school and go missing on their way home.

In Nottingham I don't face the brutality
of an occupation.
My walks through the city are safe,
full of people gazing through the noise.

This noise does not trigger traumas of genocide.

The word 'Azad' translates to freedom
from one coloniser's language to another.

Azad Kashmir?

Kashmiris remain:
Dehumanised,
displaced,
oppressed.

I'm told I shouldn't tell people
I'm Kashmiri but when I do,
they expect my silence.

The word 'Azad' translates to 'Free' in Urdu. Pakistan Administered Kashmir is referred to as 'Azad Kashmir' whereas India Occupied Kashmir is referred to as 'Jammu and Kashmir'. 'Azad' refers to freedom from Indian occupation, but Azad Kashmir is nonetheless also an example of ongoing colonisation. India Occupied Kashmir is referred to as 'Jammu and Kashmir'. This has been the subject of a dispute between India and Pakistan since 1947. 'Jammu' is recognised as a capital city in the Indian-occupied Kashmiri territories.

Man

Gazing into the window,
adoring the display of watches that
caught his eye as he walked by.
Simple pleasure. Expensive hobby.

He doesn't want game consoles
or tech gadgets.
Watches are valuable assets.

I notice his loafers and crisp slacks,
his hands hidden in the pockets
of his navy parka.
Chin tucked in, sheltered from the wind.

Leaving with a sigh, man
continues his journey.
Pulls his cap down.

Turtle Walking in Flying Horse Arcade, Nottingham

I hold my green friend on a leash as she forces each slow step. Strong winds threaten to blow my red beret away. The city is too fast for my little friend, her pace is agonising even for its empty arcades. She is not ready to walk in the shopping centre yet.

Twenty minutes feels longer. A woman sitting in the window is amused by my struggle. In between glares and whispers I gaze at paintings in the windows of art galleries. I wait for my turtle to take a step forward.

The crowd rushes ahead of us, hurries behind us. Smiling, staring, intrigued, confused. Everyone hustles from work to more work, holding coffee cups in shaky hands.

My friend and I inch into a short and narrow passage that bends left and right. Little boutiques with empty signs sit quietly. My poor little friend is trying her best, but I'm still standing here and she's out of breath. I look up at the ceiling, it is in part made of glass. CCTV cameras lurk in corners, red lights flashing.

Frustrated a little, I pick her up and walk to the café. I order my coffee. The man at the counter looks at me strangely. 'Not seen anyone take a turtle for a walk before!' He laughs. My friend retreats into her shell.

Barista

The most powerful tool
of our time
is in your hands.

This is how the world is run.

You know best how it can be used,
changed, moulded, manipulated.

A drug for crowds.
A hobby.
Release or relief.

We're in a coffee epidemic.
Without it the world would stop working.

This is how you run the world, barista.

Controlling the pulses
of caffeine withdrawal.

The Ends of The Earth

Is this where they go
when the crowd disperses?

Does the smell of the city follow
walkers to the end of the earth?

Where the threat of ecological crisis,
disease, pollution, nuclear war, and desecration…

Should I go on?

Don't mind me, I'm grappling with the thought
of looming danger as I stroll through the city centre.

My mind wanders to these places when I observe
dirty pavements and over-crowded roads.

Homeless numbers growing and overflowing bins
left open and exposed.

Walking over broken systems,
heaps of discarded waste.

Long walks to the ends of the earth.
Is it all gathered there, waiting?

Girl Talk

Simple pleasures:
Iced coffees and cake slabs.

Cafes with big windows,
full of light.

Laughing over life lessons
and imaginary situations.

Musée de l'Absence

Nudity is exposing a
paradox. Sins and gazes.
A world of conflict.
No resolution. Divide
and conquer.

Romanticise worship.
Poisoned peace from within.
Empty rooms, filled with memories.
Some muted. Others breaking
the silence.

The past is still here,
it's more present than ever.
Are they too ashamed
to pull this all from storage,
open the doors to every room?

To reveal the concealed, hidden
inside pockets and behind masks?
Everyone is welcome. See
the burned and removed.
Cancelled.

A culture that continues. Sins
and gazes. A world of conflict.
Still no resolution.
Continue:
divide and conquer.

You may remove your masks
now. It's time to redress
and re-address.
Exhibition begins 5:30pm,
blunt.

Mardi 21 Mars 2023, *Le Monde*, 3.40 €

Headline this morning reads:
"Après le 49.3, une nouvelle semaine de tensions".

Cartoon on the front page.
An empty hand reaching out
of the National Bank,
homeless person mirroring.

Economic crisis
or world crisis?

A new week of tensions.
Arrest warrant for Vladmir Putin.
Politics vs Pop Culture.
"Espresso or Cappuccino?"

Cigarettes or vapes.
Doesn't matter which
poison.

Palestine still isn't free.
World leaders are too busy
with Ukraine and TikTok.

Culture wars and culture crisis.
Time is of the essence.

Pavé

Sitting at a pavement table
across from the Seine,
distracted by the background
in everyone's selfies.

Mute the buzz.

Follow the clouds
slow motion,
sweeping the sky.

Sea blue, off white, coral
sets in above the Eiffel Tower.

Evening breeze; cigarette smoke,
vape clouds, coffee breath.
Striped shirts and white blouses.
Short haircuts and quirky hats.

Windows are open
and seats are still warm.

Unmute the bliss.

Conversations at different tables.
Somewhere amongst crowds of Parisians,
I think about how much I'd rather be

alone

with this city,
but I never am.

Le Coup de Foudre: Jardins du Luxemburg, 2 June 2022

She wins a chair by the second fountain at the Jardins du Luxemburg, among many other people. After settling in she opens her fruit pot and reaches into her tote. She pulls out a Gallimard Editions book. Her slim fingers tipped with shining nails press the iconic cream cover and red borders. She removes her bookmark and starts to read.

Her hair, highlights of caramel draping onto her shoulders like silk. Rectangular brown sunglasses mostly hidden behind loose waves, almost concealing her profile but not quite enough, exposing only the pout of her lips and the tip of her nose. She wears a brown blazer over a short white skirt, showing her sun-kissed legs. A small smile shows as she gently tucks a curl behind her ear and crosses her right leg over her left. She turns another page.

A tall man with dark hair swept back, black shades, white shirt and linen trousers towers over her confidently. She pauses. Her finger stops on the middle of a page. Clouds gather above him and drops of rain begin to fall.

Paris Metro

The apparition of these faces in the crowd: Petals on a wet, black bough.
– Ezra Pound

Dark grey. Entrée.

Packedlikesardines.
Pushedandshoved.
Shuffle for space.
Get off my case, get off my case.

Search for a seat. Train is being sucked into a black
hole. Side to side. Fast   Forward.
Light at the other end of the tunnel.
Get off my case, get off my case.

On and off.
People standing slide,
left and right.
Get off my case, get off my case.

Others leap from seats,
push through. Suit jackets, coat jackets, coats like
duvets they struggled to leave this morning.
Get off my case, get off my case.

Briefcases, backpacks, iPhones and Kindles.
Constantly switching places. Stop. By. Stop.

BEEP
BEEP
BEEP

Rushforthedoorandmindthe   gap.

Still dark grey. Sortie.

Rue

Bakeries and bars, antique shops
next to bookshops with coffee tables,
for 'café à emporter' and 'café pour rester'.
Art galleries, pedestrians coming
and going.

The sound of heels tapping concrete,
one after another. Tap, tap. Taptaptap.
Tap tap. The rhythm of pedestrians hurrying
between pavements.

Strangers brushing shoulders.
They all squeeze into the narrowspace
between
red, cream, silver, Fiat 500's, all parked.
Cycles and motorbikes,
lining up like a European cliché.

How many rues do you think make up Paris?

Red Chairs

Last night, when I opened my window, I watched the top of the Eiffel Tower glitter and glow, a luminous gold covered in white sparkles. Like small jewels, red and white lights flickered from the first floor. The perfect backdrop for white walls with black rooftops. Parisian windows, iron balconies, people enjoying a cool breeze and wine with dinner. The street below was noisy with traffic, filled pavement tables, and pedestrians looking for empty red chairs.

As the sun rose this morning, I opened my curtains to a grey sky. The Eiffel Tower doesn't sparkle in the morning. It's brown, iron, rusting. Rain tricks over it. I put on my coat and poke my head outside the window, watching the young waiter across the road put out the red chairs. He looks up with a serious face and nods at me. I nod back and smile. It always rains when I leave Paris.

Arab Quarter, Marseille

I recognise Muslim men and women everywhere.
I walk through the market
but don't attempt to buy anything.

My first query in English about a bag,
highlights that I'll be given tourist prices
even if I use my accented French.

Tables spread with
herbs and vegetables,
local and Mediterranean.

Pastèque, citron, grenade.

People shouting over market stalls,
all part of the flurry. Crowded pavement,
messy stalls.

A beige curtain. A marquee in the centre,
people sit at tables with teas and coffees.
A patisserie on the other side.

I order a Moroccan tea and baklava -
a nice change from Parisian pastries.
Voices drift in and out.

Hidden under the electric buzzing
of motorbikes and street pans sizzling,
behind me, someone clicks their lighter.

An old lady glances at me suspiciously,
possibly because my hair is not covered
and I ordered in English.

The waiter brings my tea.
The comforting fusion of black tea leaves, mint,
and sugar.

I watch the young men across the street
standing by their elders on a corner drinking coffee,
playing games, trying to sell packets of cigarettes.

The smell of tobacco slowly passes through warm air.

Parc du Champ de Mars

It is not given to everyone to blend into the multitude: Enjoying the crowd is an art. – Charles Baudelaire, 'The Crowd'

Holding a green box of macarons, you find a bench on the left side of the park. The sky is tainted yellow as the sun sinks behind the Eiffel Tower. You are waiting for someone or something. You're enjoying listening to the young man singing acoustic versions of songs to his friends on the grass. Groups of youngsters gather on small blankets, opening bottles of wine and champagne. You're amused by Parisian champagne picnics. The air suddenly became cooler, but you haven't brought a shawl. You look in your bag, it's not there. Everyone is huddling together but you, shuffling through your bag, sat on the bench with your little green box sitting on your lap. 10pm: The white sparks of light flicker, every gaze entranced. The Eiffel Tower sizzles from tip to floor, and you watch from the park bench, alone.

Rue St Honoré

"Soyez Passionné! Que cela vous concerne ou non."[1]

Take to the streets, march on.
This is who we are, all for one and one for all.

"Être Parisien, c'est être militant."[2]

The feeling of bodies. Falling
– pushed by police.
The rush of feethuddledintoroads. Vite Vite!

Slow.
Slow.

Street cobbles covered by feet warmed from marching.
Voices muted by fake news.
The media blacks out protesters' boards.

"Se taire ou être réduit au silence."[3]

Activists and radicals,
freedom fighters and free spirits.

"Nous sommes de fiers révolutionnaires."[4]

Don't dress like we're told to.
Don't think like we're told to.
Bodies used to patch up a Paris –

divided.

There is always a room for you in Paris,
but remember

 "La manière Française ou rester en denhors de notre chemin."[5]

---

[1] *Be passionate! Whether it concerns you or not.*
[2] *Being Parisian is being an activist.*
[3] *To stay silent or to be silenced.*
[4] *We were proud of our revolution.*
[5] *The French way or stay out of our way.*

Cession of Colonialism

I

You keep changing my coats
and swapping dreams for prayers.

I am floating in a lucid state.

In this space there are trees
with twisted trunks and misplaced
buckets.

Roots have been ripped out
of the soil and weeds have
grown tall.

I haven't lost track of the number of days
that I've been here, but now I talk to the trees
about them.

II

As you try to make me break my fasts,
you keep breaking your promises.

This promised land is called radical.
Rebellious.
Non-human.

But everyone here is alive and sane.

These are not forgotten people.
These are not forgotten lands.

Ceasefire. Ceasefire. Ceasefire.

Galata Bridge

Sunny June morning, 10am.
The city crowd begins to buzz.
Hustle and bustle, get ready
for the holiday rush.

People passing left and right,
cars beeping, trams and buses
pinging.

Tourists try to find a clear spot, pictures
are taken with the Bosporus Bridge.
Mosque domes and minarets towering
in the background.

The perfect social media post: small clouds
and seagulls sweeping over
the charm of Istanbul.

Old men on foldable chairs and little boys
on plastic stools. Buckets of bait
and fish food, bags with their daily essentials.
They are talking amongst themselves.

Their fishing rods lean against
the bridge arches. Fisher hats shield heads
from afternoon sun.

Steam carried into air
from chai glasses on round
copper trays.

Taksim

I sit outside the mosque
and wait for the call to prayer.

When one call stops,
another starts.

It is time for Maghrib.

Ferries pull into the port
behind the mosque.

Crowds make their way
inside to pray.

Mahgrib is the fourth prayer of the day, which takes place at sunset.

21,000 Steps

Every morning both feet meet on the prayer mat.
One beside the other.

Find a pavement. Between mosques and squares,
between streets and crowds, cars and karts,
up steep hills and down cobbled roads.

The call to prayer starts in the Hagia Sophia Mosque
and stops. It continues at the Süleymaniye Mosque.
Passing between streets that surround mosque walls,
from the minarets that tower over the city.

Crowds on their way to pray in congregation,
shoulder to shoulder. Feet meet on the prayer mat,
then disperse into Istanbul's streets.

Cats stroll, from door to table,
home to home. From crowd to crowd.
From day to night.
Repeat.

Every night both feet meet on the prayer mat.
One beside the other.

10km from Syria

The first part of a mini-Umrah.
Wandering, strolling, stepping over
white stone floors and past beige brick walls,
through narrow streets and alleys,
in the footsteps of Prophets and Saints.

I touch the gold tap, turning it slowly,
water gushing into the stone basin.
I reach my hands into the holy water.
Cooling.
One hand brushes the other.

I cup my hands and bow to take a sip.

Strolling through dusty streets.
I look up at tall marble pillars,
minarets,
hills that surround the mosque's dome.
I touch stone walls, what should l feel?

Visitor. Traveller.

Sitting in the mosque.
Praying. Listening. Watching.

Umrah, in Arabic, means 'a visit' and/or 'pilgrimage' to the Holy Kaaba (the Sacred House of God) and can be performed by a Muslim individual at any time of the year, unlike Hajj, which is an obligatory pilgrimage to Makkah performed at a specific time every year. Although I have not visited the Holy Kaaba, the journey between Konya and Halfeti (which many other pilgrims visit) became a spiritual pilgrimage for me, hence I refer to it as a 'mini-Umrah'.

Beşiktaş Port

Outside Ortakoy Cami people talk, some standing, some sitting on benches, whilst children run around the mosque. The dome and minarets are lit yellow and coral, contrasting against an indigo sky, dark navy, purple, lilac.

Music floods out of cafés and restaurants, small shops and market stalls. Boats pass by on the Bosphorus carrying parties, disco lights and pumping sound onto land. The smells of fried food and shisha smoke pass from one rooftop to the next.

Helium balloons rise on strings clutched in little hands. Ornaments and dream catchers hang next to prayer beads, and rows of tapestry and pottery are stacked on the floor below. Turn the corner, follow the path which bends from the port into narrow streets and back around again.

Cami = Mosque

Little Shops

Hidden in streets, you might miss them
if they didn't have their tables and stools outside.
Signs slanting, rusting away, have no use here.
Rows of identical tall beige buildings, paint chipped,
white wires dangling across small square windows.

A sign on the back of a scooter parked outside a shop reads:
'OTO YIKANA'.
Take a seat on colourful chairs, bright woven threads.
Simit or Gözleme, Kavesi or Chai.
The chipped marble tiles expose the grey concrete below.

A boy walks from one shop to another, balancing a big tray
of fresh Simit on one hand and munching his personal
stash of crusts with the other. He hops along in his tight polo shirt,
his belly sticking out and his sandals flip-flopping.

He cleans his mouth and shouts his salaam to the old man in the shop.
Invited in, he wipes his feet. The old man was expecting him.

'Simit' is a type of Turkish bread. It looks like a bagel and has a sweet taste. It is covered with white sesame seeds. 'Gözleme' is a type of street food. It consists of fried bread filled with spinach and cheese or potatoes or meat. 'Kavesi' is Turkish coffee. 'Chai' is Turkish tea.

Roasted Pistachios

A man walks by with a tray
of freshly baked baklava.

The smell of roasted pistachios
lingers behind him.

Enchanted. I follow.

He offers me a piece with a big
smile, excited to meet a foreigner.

Pulling out a blue stool,
he gestures me to sit down.

The plastic fork goes straight through
its pastry and pistachio stuffing.

The smell of roasted pistachios
remains in my hair when I walk away.

Man Outside Coffee Shop

Man, sitting,
legs crossed at his table.

Arms folded,
coffee cup half full.
Foot tapping.

He is lost in his thoughts,
listening to the café music.

Tawaf in Lockdown

I feel like I'm doing tawaf outside my house every day.
But it's not Mecca, it's Nottingham.
It's 2020 and the world's in lockdown.
There are no pilgrims walking with me.

Someone's just got married,
had a baby, moved into a new house,
changed the lights on their windows.
Put banners on their door,

"Congrats!"
"Happy Birthday!"

The same hill, the empty lane, no cars moving,
people walking with pets, or sometimes alone.
The Co-op and Sainsbury's are open,
the queues go all the way down the pavement.

People forget about social distancing.
Masks on, stand in your circles. Follow the arrows.

Signs that life is still changing, moving forward.
I walk up and down the same hill every day.
I sit on the same bench, halfway point.
Watch the trees. The bare branches.

Swaying…

There is no traffic to observe,
human, mechanical, or otherwise.
Sometimes people walk, the same as me.
Maybe they're doing their own tawafs.

Places from these walks are starting to seep
into my poems, my dreams, my prayers.

Tawaf is one of the principal rites of the pilgrimage and refers to circumambulating or walking in circles around the Kaaba in an anticlockwise motion.

Cyber Flâneuserie

Static. Fingers swiping over faces.
Interface and cosmetic surgery,
pictures filtered, edited, controlled.
Losing control.

App store acclaimed surgeon.
This download was recommended.
Slim bridge noses.
The online world is the only reality.

Time means something different now.

Static. Breathing through the phone speaker.
Storytelling on social media has become
ten second video clips and boomerangs.
Lip-syncing trending songs,
lined and filled with gloss.

Constant transactions.

Scrolling masked users, insecurities, AI aesthetic.
Poor credit score balances, influencer points
per label. No returns offline.
Everything held in your own hands.

Ghost City

Shut
down.

Lock
down.

Empty
                                                                        roads.

The old man walking his dog   looks at me suspiciously.
Walking on the other   side of the pavement.

There's   pavement, parking spaces, path, road   between us.
There are   facemasks, silicone gloves, social distancing   between us.

Arched eyebrows.
Did he say 'hello'?   I can't tell.
Should I ask if he's okay?   I can't tell.

Weather is getting warmer.
There's shade on this   side of the pavement.

                                    I stand outside a café that
                              I would usually be sitting inside.

I think of coffees I have drunk on the   other side of the window.

Before they turned the sɹıɐɥɔ əpısdn
uʍop and the lights went out.

Shut
down.

Lock
down.

CLOSED FOR BUSINESS.

                                                     Walk home quietly.
I cross the road
                                                         [pavement].

Queues
outside
Tesco.
Toilet paper,
and flour
shortage.
Empty   shelves.
Arrows on the floor point ⟶
Follow them.
One way only.

Shop online.
Stay inside.   One family per bubble.   In silence.
Worry anxiously about tomorrow.
News announcement at 6 PM. BBC ONE.

                 Everyone meets in the living room.
Avoid leaving the house.
Nothing changes for a while.
Front doors.

CLOSED FOR FRIENDS.

Inside our lockdown homes
we live with the ghosts
of our pre-pandemic lives.

Shut
down.

Lock
down.

A Hashtag

I am #Trending.
#HotTopic. #UK.
Conform or leave.
Fit this box.
Permission to create your own,
denied.

War in 2024

The party told you to reject the evidence of your eyes and ears. It was their final, most essential command – George Orwell (1984)

I can only speak in poetry.
I was taught only to write in prose.
I've performed for whoever will listen,
but I've fallen short of speeches.

In my dreams I scrunch sheets of paper
to make rocks that I hurl at colonisers.

I watch them bounce off men in blue masks;
the rocks fly towards me in slow motion instead.

Leaving cuts. Red. Wet. Dripping.
Hands covered in bruises.

When poetry is a form of resistance
words are the bricks that build
homes on landslides of desecration.

Take my poem from me.

Colonisers enjoy poetry about
flowing rivers and deep blue seas.
Anything they can conquer and destroy next.

You don't need fresh stems to write for liberation.
Colonisers are interested in roots.

They try to force us to forget, but this is not
the history we choose for ourselves.

Instagram Captions
(@thepostcolonialflaneuse)

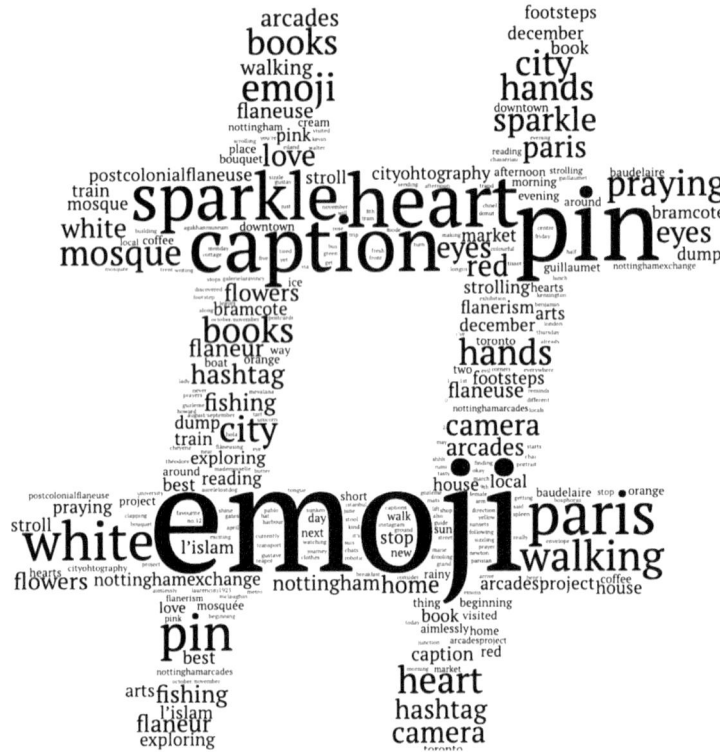

Acknowledgements

بِسْمِ ٱللَّهِ ٱلرَّحْمَٰنِ ٱلرَّحِيمِ

In the name of Allah, The Most Compassionate, The Most Merciful.

All praise is due to Allah, the Lord of all worlds.

I am grateful first to Allah. Without His mercy and blessing writing these poems would not be possible.

Thank you to my mum for inspiring me to be the woman I am today and for always showing up and believing in me. Thank you for your endless prayers and protection.

Thank you to Andrew Taylor, for your warmth, creative mentorship and honest advice which I will always treasure, and for encouraging me to submit my poems to this call for pamphlets.

Thank you to Jenni Ramone for your unwavering support, invaluable mentorship and kind friendship. Your guidance has shaped the academic I have become and the one I hope to be.

Thank you to Rory Waterman, Tim Youngs, and Andrew Thacker for sharing encouraging words of advice and expertise, reading recommendations, and your time so generously.

Thank you to my good friend Paul Adey for teaching me through example that creativity is a way of life.

Thank you to Suhaiymah Manzoor-Khan for constantly inspiring me and offering your time and friendship with such generosity.

Thank you to my family and friends for surrounding me with the inspiration and love that carries me through.

Thank you to the British Association for Islamic Studies (BRAIS), Postcolonial Studies Association (PSA), NTU Research for Travel Writing Centre, NTU Postcolonial Research Group, and NTU Global for awarding me funding that supported the trips during which I wrote many of the poems included in this pamphlet.

Thank you to Pippa Hennessy of Five Leaves for your patience and guidance throughout the editing and publication process of this pamphlet.

Thank you to all the Muslim women, poets and writers who have paved the way. Hanan Issa, Naush Sabah, Rakhshan Rizwan, Safia Khan, and Suma Din for your allyship and encouragement. Ruby Hamad, whose fearless work and voice remind me to keep using mine.

Thank you to the marginalised women fighting injustice in the cities and crowds all over the world. I see you, my fellow Postcolonial Flâneuses.

Five Leaves New Poetry

Five Leaves presents a new series of debut poetry pamphlets by East Midlands writers, showcasing the exciting range of emerging talent from our region.

1. *She Will Allow Her Wings* Jane Bluett
   978-1-915434-09-8, 40 pages, £7, June 2023
2. *Beyond Caring* Trish Kerrison
   978-1-915434-10-4, 40 pages, £7, September 2023
3. *North by Northnorth* Elvire Roberts
   978-1-915434-12-8, 44 pages, £7, December 2023
4. *The Stories In Between* Teresa Forrest
   978-1-915434-11-1, 32 pages, £7, December 2023
5. *Keep All the Parts* Roy Young
   978-1-915434-13-5, 34 pages, £7, March 2024
6. *Relief Map* Jan Norton
   978-1-915434-14-2, 33 pages, £7, March 2024
7. *New Uses for a Wand* Fiona Theokritoff
   978-1-915434-16-6, 40 pages, £7, June 2024
8. *You Worry Too Much* Nathan Fidler
   978-1-915434-17-3, 32 pages, £7, June 2024
9. *Kindling* Julie Burke
   978-1-915434-19-7, 44 pages, £7, September 2024
10. *Remembering* Julie Gardner
    978-1-915434-20-3, 40 pages, £7, September 2024
11. *Full Body Reclaim* Caroline Stancer
    978-1-915434-25-8, 40 pages, £7, December 2024
12. *Rainbow Candles* Tony Challis
    978-1-915434-31-9, 40 pages, £7, September 2025
13. ✸ *Fr⇕gm∞nts* ⊗ Tara Singh
    978-1-915434-32-6, 40 pages, £7, September 2025
14. *The Postcolonial Flâneuse* Ramisha Rafique
    978-1-915434-33-3, 52 pages, £7, November 2025
15. *Balancing Act* Elizabeth Dunford
    978-1-915434-34-0, 40 pages, £7, November 2025
16. *Familiar Phantoms* Sue Forrester
    978-1-915434-35-7, 40 pages, £7, November 2025

All pamphlets can be ordered from our websites.

Five Leaves Publications/Bookshop
14a Long Row, Nottingham NG1 2DH
info@fiveleaves.co.uk
www.fiveleaves.co.uk

0115 837 3097
bookshop@fiveleaves.co.uk
www.fiveleavesbookshop.co.uk